MASHIACH

Hope for Turbulent Times

Questions and Answers
About the Jewish Messiah

The Dr. Eleonora Goudis Edition
A Breslov Woman Publication
By Chaya Rivka Zwolinski

DEDICATIONS

In loving memory of my mother Chana bat Ephraim

Despite growing up in the Soviet Union, my mother epitomized Emunah (faith) in Hashem and instilled in her children, grandchildren and great-grandchildren the importance of Emunah and gratitude. She was a woman who was full of life and incredibly devoted to her family. She set an example to all of us as a Jewish woman, mother, grandmother and amazing person! Her memory will forever be cherished.

On behalf of my whole family, I'd like to express our deepest appreciation to everyone whose generosity helped this priceless project come to fruition. I am deeply touched by the kindness of everyone who has helped keep my mother's memory alive through the publication of this book. A very special thank you to Chaya Rivka. Thank you for sharing your Emunah with us.

Every time someone reads this book on Mashiach and the Redemption, may it be an Aliyah for the neshama of Chana bat Ephraim.

L'iluy nishmat Chana bat Ephraim,
beloved mother of Eleonora Goudis
Alex and Ella Gurevich

L'iluy nishmat and in loving memory
of Chana bat Ephraim
The Frenkel Family, Marina, Feliks,
Bobby & Gabi, and Ariel

In memory of Chana bat Ephraim,
Lia Leybzon and Alexander Friedman

For an aliyah for the neshama of Chana bat Ephraim
Irene and Simon Shevelev

In Honor of Chana bat Ephraim, beloved
mother of Eleonora Goudis
The Belkin Family

In memory of Chana bat Ephraim
Nina, Alex, Gaby & Danny Paltag, Patsy, Alex
& Victoria Palag, and Tamara Paltag

L'iluy Nishmat Chana bat Ephraim
When a person reads a teaching about the
Redemption and is inspired, a spark of the Mashiach
is activated. May these sparks light the way for the
coming of Mashiach, and be a merit for Chana bat
Ephraim, beloved mother of Eleonora Goudis.
Gavriel Gedalya and Chana Sneider,
President of Breslov Woman

This book is dedicated in honor and memory of Chana
bat Ephraim, beloved mother of Dr. Eleonora Goudis.
The Jewish Messiah and the Redemption will
bring peace to the Jewish people and the entire
world. It is the hope of the author that everyone
who reads this book finds inspiration, faith and
hope in these pages, and may it be an aliyah
for Chana bat Ephraim's holy neshama.
Chaya Rivka Zwolinski, Director, Breslov Woman

TABLE OF CONTENTS

Will I change as a person after Mashiach comes? Will I be able to work and maintain my standard of living after Mashiach is revealed? I love my home. Will I be required to move to the Land of Israel?

What will happen in the Holy Temple in Jerusalem? Why does the Temple have to be in Jerusalem?

The third Temple and Redemption is a future prediction. Have any past predictions related to the Temple and Redemption come true? After Mashiach comes will people still get sick? Will they die? What about the resurrection of the dead? Is it just a metaphor or a real event? What will Mashiach teach me? What will my relationships be like, including my relationship with Hashem? What can you do to prepare yourself for personal, spiritual change?

How should I prepare for what may likely be a very sudden arrival of the Mashiach and the Redemption? The delights of the Geulah are tempting, but it seems like there is so much to learn. What can I do if I want to progress without being overwhelmed? What is the main thing to focus on?

INTRODUCTION

Do you have a sense that the world is racing towards an unavoidable turning point? That's because, according to thousands of years of Jewish wisdom, it is. We are seeing the evidence with our own eyes. Since the publication of the first edition of this book, Israel has been under attack, and antisemitism is on the rise. Jews are being verbally and physically attacked in the streets of Israeli, American and European cities.

In general, people are more polarized than ever before. What are they arguing about? The economy, racism, the global pandemic (vaccination, masks, policy), climate change, Israel and the Middle East, national and international politics, and more. Parents and students are finding it difficult to cope with swift and dramatic changes to the educational/intellectual landscape and in many cases, educators and parents are on opposite sides. The legacy media seems to be dying a slow death as many people turn to independent sources for their news, making it easier than ever for people to access both accurate and inaccurate information.

Depending on where you live, work, worship and what media you consume, you may believe that the economy is being strangled by pointless policies or you may believe that government regulations haven't gone far enough. In some cities, local governments are still enforcing economically-crippling laws put in place during the height of the Covid-19 pandemic while many small and medium-sized businesses have closed their doors forever. We're also seeing prices of gas, food, lumber and other goods skyrocket.

Of those who practice their religion, most agree that policies that clamp down on freedoms, especially those involving religion and free speech, have been ascendent during the past fifteen years. (Politicians seem to prioritize nearly every right except the right to freedom of religion.) Invectives are being hurled in the public sphere, as usual, but "cancel culture" is now an effective weapon of the intolerant. On the emotional front, despite online get-togethers, people are experiencing an unprecedented sense of isolation. Statistics appear to show that depression and anxiety disorders are on the rise. It seems like more people are lonely and afraid than ever before. It is an uncomfortable, even frightening time for many.

This book is a response to these turbulent times we live in.

Today it seems that most people yearn to know what will happen in the immediate and long-term future and how best to prepare. People like you and me also want to know what is going on, from a deeper, spiritual perspective, and how the coming changes will affect us. It's also a time when many people are openly talking and asking questions about the Mashiach (Messiah) and the future of humanity.

The truth is, many people believe in God and believe in His special relationship with the Jewish people, but have sincere questions and doubts about the Mashiach and the world-wide Redemption. They find it difficult to believe in or envision the Redemption because they have never learned much about it. Others are turned off by confusing pronouncements put forth by some about the Mashiach's identity, some of which directly contradict authentic Jewish teachings.

Many more are turned off to the idea of the Messiah because they mistakenly believe the concept comes from other religions. But it's the other way around; the nations of the world took this completely Jewish concept, that of the Messiah, twisted it into a pretzel of confusing ideas and entwined it with idol worship. The result? We've been afraid to talk about the Mashiach ever since.

All of this confusion also makes us feel squeamish about asking questions. Yet the questions persist. The goal of this book is to as succinctly as possible answer the basic questions you have about the coming of the Mashiach and the Geulah (the world-wide Redemption). This book aims to provide an elementary understanding which you can use as a jumping-off point to other studies in this topic.

Originally printed as a special limited-edition in honor and memory of Chana bat Ephraim, beloved mother of Dr. Eleonora Goudis, the positive response from readers of *Mashiach: Hope for Turbulent Times*, has been unprecedented. Now, this updated version is being published and offered for sale in order to make it more widely-available.

To help make this book easy to navigate, there are six chapters, each presented in a question-and-answer format, so you can quickly find the answers to the questions most important to you. Chapter titles are in the form of questions and related, italicized questions are included as sub-headings in each chapter. The material in this book relies on straightforward explanations of widely-accepted, authentic Jewish sources and therefore endnotes are provided so you further explore the source material yourself. Also included is a glossary of terms. To help you learn more about this topic, there is also short list of suggested reading, both online and print. Rather than just publish this book electronically, we felt it was important to produce an inexpensive paperback version you can carry with you in your pocket or purse, and easily gift to friends and acquaintances.

It is my sincere wish that this little book inspires you to explore more of our rich Jewish teachings about the Mashiach, the Geulah, and our faith, and that it begins to answer the questions you have about Mashiach, but were afraid (or embarrassed) to ask. Most of all, may it offer comfort and hope, please God, to everyone who reads it.

With joy,
Chaya Rivka Zwolinski
Iyar, 5781- May, 2021

CHAPTER ONE

What will (my) life be like after Mashiach comes?

Will I change as a person after Mashiach comes?

Each person will change and grow spiritually after Mashiach comes (but this doesn't preclude the necessity of growing and working on ourselves now)! We could even say that a significant piece of Mashiach's work will be to help each of us change, using his special, spiritual abilities. How? Descriptions of Mashiach are found in the book of Isaiah in Prophets[*]: When the "shoot of Jesse" is revealed, the "spirit of God" will rest on him. He will have a spirit of wisdom and understanding, a spirit of wise advice and heroism, a spirit of knowledge and awe of God. He will evaluate every person using these talents and his refined, spiritually-keen sense of "smell."

---

[*] It's important to note that when reading a translation of Isaiah, or anything from Tanakh (the Hebrew Bible), it's essential to read a genuine Jewish translation with authentic Jewish commentary to avoid misinterpretations and mistranslations by non-Jewish sources.

The Tzaddikim teach us that the wise powers of evaluation possessed by Mashiach will enable him to help each person find his personal tikkun, his true soul-correction and individualized soul-healing path. When we heal our souls, we will be better able to embrace the era of peace and closeness to the Divine that the Mashiach will usher in. He will gather in all the Jews and help us vanquish our enemies, both internal and external. The Holy Temple will be rebuilt and we will stream to it. All types of idolatry will dissolve. (Some of the idolatry we commonly encounter today isn't the worship of idols or statues, but rather the worship of money, power, fame, status, and so on.) As part of the soul-healing process, Mashiach will also teach each of us to truly connect to the Creator through meditative prayer. This type of personal prayer, called hitbodedut*, is something many people already do today, and is accessible to everyone.

---

* Hitbodedut, also known as personal prayer, is a prayerful, talking meditation in which you speak and truly open up to the Creator, talking about whatever is on your mind and in your heart. This is the original form of prayer before the Sanhedrin created the prayer services we find in the siddur. Daily hitbodedut is as central to life as a Jew, as prayer from a siddur at home or in synagogue. (Your great-grandparents and all your ancestors most likely spoke to God many times a day.)

*Will I be able to work and maintain my standard
of living after Mashiach is revealed?*

The time of Mashiach will likely be a succession of
time-periods of ever-increasing miracles. Especially after
the third Holy Temple is built in Jerusalem, your financial
stresses will be alleviated and you will earn or receive
your income much more easily, which will free up your
time for spiritual development (and others will come to
serve you and take care of all your needs.)[1] As the coarse
materialism of the world fades and the spirituality which
is now hidden is revealed, physical needs such as the
need for food, will be met more and more miraculously
over time.

*I love my home. Will I be required to
move to the Land of Israel?*

Most if not all Jews will return to the Holy Land (Israel/
Zion): "And the redeemed of Zion shall return, and they
shall come to Zion with song, with joy of days of yore
shall be upon their heads; they shall achieve gladness and
joy, and sadness and sighing shall flee."[2] Some say that
during the initial stages of the Geulah, this move might
happen little by little, others say there will be a dramatic
influx of the exiles. There are some who say that only those
Jews who are working on developing their spirituality/
connection to God and genuinely want to make Aliyah
will do so. Still, nearly everyone will flock to the Holy
Temple in Jerusalem for the festivals. Eventually Jerusalem,
which today is ripe with the world's greatest extant and
potential holiness, will expand to fill up the entire Land

of Israel. And Israel itself will expand to fill up the entire world![3] Though most Jews will want to live in the Holy Land, the central place of Jewish spirituality where each soul can flourish, if anyone does remain outside, it may still be possible to find some level of purity, holiness and spiritual connection in those places.

What will happen in the Holy Temple in Jerusalem?

The Beit Hamikdash, the Holy Temple, is the concentration point of the holiest technology the world has ever seen. When operated as intended (through the various Temple services and offerings), it radiates holiness throughout Israel and the world, in what we might describe as a spiritual nuclear fusion of Heaven and Earth. The third Temple, the one that will be built in the times of the Mashiach (by the Mashiach or possibly built in the Heavens and sent down to earth or a combination of both) will hold great attraction for every Jew, including the simplest among us. Righteous non-Jews will also be attracted to the Temple which "shall be called a House of Prayer for all nations."[4]

Why does the Temple have to be in Jerusalem?

The reasons why Mt. Moriah, the location of the Temple, is so important is that it is considered to be the navel of the world, the foundation stone, from which God fashioned the earth. In that place various offerings and animal sacrifices were made and prayers went (and will go) straight up to God. It is the place where Adam, Cain and Abel, and Noah offered sacrifices. It's the place where

Abraham prepared to sacrifice Isaac and where Jacob had his vision of the angels and the ladder.

At another special location, Mount Sinai, the nascent Jewish people were commanded to build a sanctuary so God could dwell among them.[5] Under Moshe's leadership, the Jews built the Ark of the Covenant, and carried it with them on their wanderings. Eventually the ark made its way to Jerusalem where King David built an altar on Mount Moriah, and where eventually, King Solomon built the first Temple (and where the Jews together with Herod built the second one.)

There is a special holiness at the site of the Temple, the place we call today the Temple Mount, which includes the area where the Arabs have their mosque. The future Temple (like the previous two) will be of a highly-detailed, complex and beautiful design, which will belie the laws of Newtonian physics.[6] The fundamental spiritual quality of the Beit Hamikdash is that it is a dwelling place for God's presence on earth. The energy at the site of the Temple is conducive to the meeting of human and Divine.

The third Temple and Redemption is a future prediction. Have any past predictions related to the Temple and Redemption come true?

There are many Biblical prophecies regarding the Temple and the Geulah that have already come true, such as the beginning of the ingathering of the exiles. Today, for the first time in 2000 years, more Jews live in Israel than in any other land. Also, as predicted, the city of Jerusalem has been destroyed and rebuilt nine times, the Holy Temple has been destroyed twice and so far, rebuilt once. Perhaps the most poignant evidence of a prediction is the meaning embedded in King Solomon's Song of Songs, "Behold—He (Hashem) stands behind our wall…"[7] The midrash tells us that the Shechina (the hidden Divine Presence) will never leave the Kotel (the Western Wall), and therefore the Kotel will never be destroyed.[8] Today, no one who visits the Kotel remains unmoved; the presence of eternal holiness is palpable.

After Mashiach comes will people still get sick? Will they die?

The good news is that eventually, death will no longer occur: Hashem "will swallow up death forever."[9]. When Adam was created, his soul was greater than his physical body, but today, the needs of our physical bodies often take precedence. After Mashiach is revealed, although there will be a period during which sickness as we know it might not exist, people will die. However, after some period of time, some say 40 years, a period of higher spirituality and greater miracles will begin. "Then the eyes of the blind shall be opened, and the ears of the deaf shall be unstopped. Then the lame shall skip like a hart, and the tongue of the mute shall sing, for water has broken out in the desert and streams in the plain. And they shall say on that day, "Behold, this is our God: we hoped for Him that He would save us; this is the Lord for Whom we hoped; let us rejoice and be happy with His salvation."[10]

What about the resurrection of the dead?
Is it just a metaphor or a real event?

The final principle of Rambam's (Maimonides) 13 Foundations of Faith is the belief in the resurrection of the dead. For some this can be a troubling principle (one student told me that she envisioned "zombies.") But what we know about this resurrection is actually very hopeful and positive. The Tanakh tells us that at some point after the preliminary Messianic period, the dead will come to life and inhabit their bodies, which will be reconstructed from a special "seed" bone called the luz bone, which is at the very tip of our spine. (Some compare it to a stem cell.) If you have ever cooked with dried beans (which are actually a type of dried seed) or planted a garden from seed, you know that there are a few special seeds in each batch that are small and very hard and which can survive intact under the most challenging conditions. If there is a time of ecological disaster, these seeds might survive for years, even decades. In fact, some can survive millennia. In 2005 an Israeli doctor planted a few 2000-year-old date palm seeds (the most intact of several she had found)—and they germinated! Today those palm trees are still standing.

Akin to a seed, the indestructible tiny luz bone contains the recipe for our resurrection, and in the Hand of the Creator, it will be used to resurrect the righteous who have died, "You will revive me again and bring me up from the depths of the earth."[11] Our family members who've already passed away will be brought back to life, too. It is said that any Jew who returns to Hashem will be resurrected, will live on at the next level of existence, and experience a state of bliss.

What will Mashiach teach me?

Some of Mashiach's goals and achievements are discussed throughout this mini-book. We might consider his main achievement to be to teach each Jew how to truly connect to and develop awareness of God. We will intensify our gratitude to God and thank Him and sing His praises. Mashiach may also show righteous non-Jews how they can serve God, too. The Mashiach will eagerly and lovingly give over his knowledge in a way that builds us up and instills in us the belief that we are truly capable of great goodness.

Inside each of us is a spark of the Divine, a Godly soul, that is completely good. Rebbe Nachman of Breslov teaches that each Jew has this good point which is the Godly soul inside.[12] This good point also can be compared to a "spark of Mashiach."[13] In other words, you have a spark of the Mashiach in you! No matter how difficult your personal journey is, no matter how low you feel, no matter how confused and heavy is your heart, there is still a spark of holiness inside you which, if unleashed, has the potential to light up the world. Today, in the times before Mashiach is revealed, each of us can learn to build what I call Holy Self Esteem by learning the teachings of the true Tzaddikim, especially Rebbe Nachman's teachings on this subject (see Azamra in Appendix B.) In order to reveal your personal spiritual greatness, you'll need to believe yourself truly capable of spiritual greatness, and equally important, you'll need to walk your path of personal growth with *joy*.

The Rambam teaches: And at that time there will be no hunger or war, no jealousy or rivalry. For the good will be plentiful, and all delicacies as commonly available as the dust. The entire occupation of the world will be only to know God… Israel will be of great wisdom; they will perceive the esoteric truths and comprehend their Creator's wisdom as is the capacity of man. As it is written: "For the land shall be filed with the knowledge of God, as the waters cover the sea…"[14]

What will my relationships be like, including my relationship with Hashem?

During the Messianic era, the world will be filled with knowledge of Hashem. Mashiach (and other tzaddikim) will help fill our minds and hearts with this knowledge. Each person will have their own level of holy knowledge and awareness of the Creator. The difficult relationships in your life (past relationships included) will be able to be healed. We'll all see we are truly "on the same side" and eventually anger, jealousy and hurt will become things of the past. You'll see how each encounter you've have had in your life, whether it was a brief acquaintanceship or a life-long relationship, arose to teach you something about life and about yourself. You will experience more forgiveness and a greater ability to have compassion for others and vice versa.

As for your relationship with Hashem, that will continue to grow. Even now, you have implanted in you the potential to have a relationship with God, to truly love Him and even yearn to be closer to Him. Perhaps until now, Hashem has loved you more than you love Him. The love between Hashem and each person mostly comes from God's side because only He is truly capable of this ultimate Love. Still, Judaism is replete with teachings that describe this love for Hashem that you personally are capable of developing and will develop further in the Messianic age.

King David describes his love and desire for Hashem in so many different ways in Psalms. Reading his words can inspire you, for example: *One thing I ask of Hashem, this is what I will seek: That I dwell in the House of Hashem all the days of my life, to behold the sweetness of Hashem and to experience His Sanctuary.*[15]

And, *For the Lord is good, His lovingkindness is forever; He is faithful to generation after generation.*[16]

Other Torah passages also offer us descriptions of this mutual love. You love Hashem like a father and Hashem loves you like a child: *You are children to Hashem, your God.*[17]

Not only is God holy, but you are holy to Him, and are His special treasure: *For you are a holy people to the Lord, your God, and the Lord has chosen you to be a treasured people for Him.*[18]

The relationship between Hashem and his people is even compared to husband to wife: *Let him kiss me with the kisses of his mouth, for your love is better than wine.*[19]

Hashem knows you. He created you. He knows your thoughts. Wherever you are, He is there. Think about the closest relationships in your life—spouse, children, siblings, parents, dear friends. One of the hallmarks of those relationships is your knowledge of the beloved and your beloved's knowledge of you. Without knowledge of the other, there cannot be true love. When the earth is filled with knowledge of Hashem, there will be true love for Hashem.

What can you do to prepare yourself for personal, spiritual change? Take some time each day to talk to God. Find a quiet spot where you won't be interrupted. You might want to begin by asking Hashem to help you talk to Him. The key to maintaining your psychospiritual equilibrium when Mashiach is revealed is to strengthen your connection to God, now.

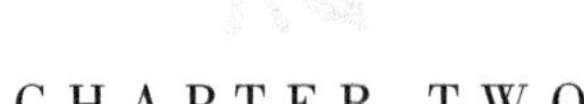

I'm interested in learning more about the Messiah, but I am more focused on the way things are going right now. Why should I think about the Mashiach when I really just want things to go back to the way they were?

More people than ever recognize that we are in the process of major change and that we must expect the unexpected. Can we really go back to thinking only about our day-to-day existence when we see the world around us changing so dramatically? Our sages tell us that there's a definitive reason to think about the coming of Mashiach: It's the entire purpose of creation. The pages of our Torah (the Hebrew Bible) are filled with stories about and revelations by the Jewish prophets and these prophecies primarily concern one thing: The Messianic era. No less a universal Jewish authority than the Ramban (Nachmanides) writes: "The end goal and purpose of all prophecies is the coming of Mashiach, as our sages have said: "All the prophets prophesied only concerning the days of Mashiach."[1] Ramban is telling us that literally everything the prophets said is related to the times of the Messiah. There is a consensus: The Messianic age is the entire end goal and purpose of creation.

If we look a bit more closely at the breadth and depth of Jewish wisdom, we find extensive discussion about this end goal and purpose of creation. Indeed, the concept of the Redemption is embedded in virtually every aspect of Jewish life. Take for example, Shabbat. The Jewish sages teach that this end goal, the Messianic era, is considered to be a great Shabbat for the entire world. Rebbe Nachman of Breslov tells us that prior to Hashem's creation of the world, He thought of Mashiach and the Geulah. In other words, Hashem's first thought prior to Creation was the coming world-wide Shabbat, the Messianic era.

We are reminded of this on Friday nights when we sing the beautiful melody, *Lecha Dodi*.[2] The lyrics refer to Shabbat as: *Last in deed, first in thought*. These words hint to the greater Shabbat of the Messianic age. Just as each week on Shabbat we can feel ourselves transported from the mundane weekday rush to a more peaceful, spiritual time, in the future, we will also experience the greater Shabbat that is the Redemption. This era will be wonderful and Hashem wants us to look forward to what's coming, so he has given us a gift: On the weekly Shabbat we get a little taste of the delights of this Olam Haba, this World to Come. Shabbat is said to be one sixtieth of Olam Haba so we are getting one sixtieth of that experience now.[3]

*What does this idea of Hashem's first
thought mean to me personally?*

The fact that God began creation, so to speak, with a "thought" can teach you something about your own thoughts. A spark of creative thought may lead you to take a creative action. In fact, every act of human creation begins with a thought. When an architect designs a house, he first thinks about and envisions the finished building standing strong and beautiful, perhaps a space in which the inhabitants can joyfully celebrate Shabbat. Only then can he begin the design process, source the materials, dig the foundation, and so on. The final building is a testament to his initial idea. When an entrepreneur has a vision of the business she wants to create, she uses the power of her imaginative thought to envision her future business and then she creates it. When a homemaker decides to bake a chocolate cake, she first thinks about the finished dessert, picturing her family eating it with delight. Only then does she buy the ingredients and mix the batter. This is true for everyone, including you. Your thoughts are literally the source and fuel of your personal creative powers. What you think about defines and even creates your reality.[4]

Thoughts of faith and belief are even more powerful. They can lift you out of depression, fear and worry, inspire you to build a family or community, and bring you closer to Hashem. Thoughts of faith can even help you learn more about your true self. Emunah (faith and belief) lends its creative power to your personal reality. We'll learn later on that having faith and believing that the Mashiach is coming is even an essential and fundamental principle of Judaism. We must have faith in and anticipate the Mashiach's coming, each and every day. And because our thoughts are so powerful that they can help create reality—thinking about Mashiach helps to bring Mashiach. But it's hard to think about and envision Mashiach and the future if you don't know what you're supposed to be anticipating or why. That's why listening to classes on the topic and reading books like this one are a good first step.

I've worked hard to attain success and I want to live "happily ever after." But now I'm worried about the unrest and upheaval. The pandemic as well as the politicization of the pandemic, the contentious election, the protests and riots, the dramatic rise in anti-Jewish hatred, are all so overwhelming—can't I just pray for things to go "back to normal?"

It's natural to want your life to go as planned. You have been working hard, to get ahead financially and to provide a good life for your family. Especially for today's first and second-generation Jewish refugees (such as those from the F.S.U., the Levant, etc.) becoming an American citizen and living in a land dedicated to liberty like the United States, was and still is a dream come true. These special Jewish immigrants worked incredibly hard to create a stable, comfortable life not only for themselves, but for their children, grandchildren and great-grandchildren. We cannot overestimate the efforts they made to learn English, study extensively and take risks. The idea that this life they worked so hard to build may not be permanent can be a genuinely frightening thought. Yet it truly seems as if the world has turned upside down. Nothing is as it was. It is a natural inclination for any person, and especially Jewish immigrants and their children, to wish life would return to "normal." But what is normal for a Jew?

There's a famous story from the Talmud that tells us what kind of "normal" we can expect in life. It is told by Rabbah bar bar Chana, who describes traveling by sea and after a while, spotting an island. He and the sailors rowed over to the island and decided to make a fire on which to cook their dinner. But as the fire heated up, the island began to tremble and shake. Finally, after a tremendous convulsion, it threw the sailors into the sea. If it weren't for the fact that they were able to swim to their ship, which was moored nearby, they would have drowned. What was the secret of this bizarre island? It wasn't an island at all! It was actually a gigantic fish, which had been resting so long that grass grew on its back, giving it the appearance of terra firma. The fish became irritated by the sailors' hot barbeque, and shook them off its back.[5]

This allegory reveals the fragility of our place as Jews in this world. We see a land. It appears good and solid. But when things heat up (recession, pandemic, war, corruption, oppressive regime change, etc.) the land is no longer a safe harbor for us. Eventually, it will toss us out, one way or another. Throughout our history of exile, we've had periods of relative calm in many lands (Persia/Iran, Iraq, Turkey, Western Europe, Morocco, etc.) and even periods during which Jews have flourished in Jewish scholarship and/or economically (the golden age of Spain., etc.) Especially in the United States, which has become the home of several generations of Jews who fled oppression for a life of freedom, our people have found safety. Here, we have enjoyed the ability to live relatively freely while openly identifying as Jews—ethnically, culturally and religiously. For many, living a life in which one's Jewish identity can play a visibly-central role, has truly felt like a miracle.

Today, much of this is under question. The stress of new living arrangements, quarantines, job and income loss, illness, lack of social gatherings, restricted travel and closed schools and synagogues, not to mention the dramatic increase in antisemitism, has affected all the important details of our everyday lives. Naturally, people yearn for how things were before. Even so, our sages teach that the yearning of a Jew is unique. While every human being wishes for the return of his safe, comfortable routine, our sages imply that for us, upheaval can be a gift. It's an opportunity for us to turn our thoughts towards God. Upheaval may motivate you to pray for personal and world-wide salvation. And when you do, you will connect to the Source of any and all relief, and the ultimate solution to all your problems—Hashem.

The key lies in the power of thought we described above. If you think about your life deeply, you most likely yearn for peace. You long to connect more sincerely and lovingly to the people in your life. You yearn to be true to your deepest self. You reflect on what it means to be a Jew and what Hashem's plans are for you and the Jewish people. You envision an end to your troubles and a life without fear or worry. When you pray and join your personal desires to a broader desire for peace and joy for the Jewish people as well as the entire world, you open yourself up to the greater connection that your soul naturally craves.

A parable sums up the crazy times we're living through and offers hope of making this connection:[6]

The Tainted Grain

Once upon a time, a worried king had a talk with his prime minister and good friend. The king said, "I can see in the stars, that every person in my kingdom who eats grain from this year's harvest is going to go mad! (The grain was tainted with ergot, a fungus which causes hallucinations.) What, dear friend, do you think we should do?"

The prime minister thought about it and came up with an idea. He told the king that perhaps they might set aside grain from last year's good-quality, undamaged harvest so they wouldn't have to eat any of the tainted grain.

"But it will be impossible to set aside enough for everyone in the kingdom," said the king. "And, if we set aside just enough grain for you and me, we'll be the only ones who aren't bonkers. Everyone else will be insane, but they'll look at us and say that you and I are the insane ones. I have a better idea. Instead, you and I will eat this year's tainted grain along with everyone else. But this is what we'll do: We'll put a sign on each of our foreheads. I will look at your forehead and you will look at my forehead. And when we see the sign, then we will remember that we are both crazy."

It seems like the entire world has already been eating the tainted grain. But each Jew is a little bit like the king and his minister. We have to look to each other—and to our sages—to recognize what's true and sane. What is the sign on the forehead? It's the study of Torah and Judaism. It's faith and belief. It's the teachings of the true Tzaddikim. It's having hope in the Mashiach's arrival. It's the one, true King Himself, God. If we remind each other who we truly are—holy Jewish souls—we won't forget that the whole world has gone crazy but we have a sign that can help us see the truth.

What can you do to stay sane and focused in this mixed-up world? Learn more about what authentic Jewish teachings have to say. Remember who you really are: a spiritual being in a physical body. Tap into the power of your thoughts by thinking about and praying for yourself and those you know. Pray for world-wide redemption.

CHAPTER THREE

I already believe in God. Is it necessary that I believe in Mashiach, too?

Shockingly, according to the Rambam (Maimonides), the belief in the Mashiach is so integral to being a Jew, that even if someone believes in Hashem and His Torah and lives accordingly, but doesn't believe in and anticipate the Mashiach and the Geulah, his faith is considered incomplete, his Judaism invalid.[1]

Yet it's not unusual for people to question whether or not they truly believe in the coming of the Messiah. But belief in the coming of Mashiach is so central to Judaism that the Rambam, who was a celebrated scholar and doctor known for his rational, practical approach to Jewish life, says that *belief in the coming of Mashiach is a requirement for every Jew.* In fact, he included this belief in his universally-accepted list of the 13 Foundations of Faith.[2] Foundation number 12 speaks about the Mashiach and how a Jew must think about him. It tells us to instill belief in Mashiach's coming in our minds and hearts: *I believe with complete faith in the coming of the Mashiach and even though he may delay, still, I anticipate his arrival every day.*

The coda to the entire 13 foundations, which is found in many prayer books, further cements the idea that the coming of Mashiach is a principle of Judaism, so much so that it states in every possible permutation the following: *For Your Salvation I yearn Hashem. I yearn, Hashem, for Your Salvation. Hashem, for Your Salvation I yearn.* The great Arizal teaches that one should yearn for the coming of Mashiach when saying these words.[3] And we understand from the juxtaposition, that true and complete Salvation from God, both on a national and personal level, comes with the Messianic age.

How can faith, belief or feelings be subject to command?

It's might be difficult to understand why thoughts and feelings are so integral to Judaism—does it really matter what you think or feel as long as you are a good person who follows the Jewish way? Let's briefly explore the different underlying philosophical approaches of Judaism vs. much of the rest of the world in order to answer this question. As Western civilization developed from its Greek roots, it transmitted the idea that an ideal society offers each person the liberty to believe—and live—mostly as he wishes. This credo developed into classical liberalism. The post-religious West took this idea and ran with it.

Until now, America has provided more personal liberty than any other nation on earth. It has offered a genuine reprieve from totalitarianism and oppression. Everybody in the West, including Jews, has been essentially free to live as he wishes. We have the free will to choose our path as Jews, but we must keep in mind our history: reprieves such as America has offered, are temporary for Jews. In America today, we see many of our social systems breaking down. In many cases, basic freedoms that we've become accustomed to, such as the freedom of speech and travel, have been squelched. Jews are reminded of what our people have experienced as a harsh reality since time immemorial: man-made social systems (even the democratic republic of the United States), no matter how noble, are eventually bound to deconstruct or decompose, because the systems are created by fallible beings. Because mankind is able to create belief systems, he is also able to destroy them. In human endeavor, entropy follows eminence. The Torah (and Judaism), though, has never wavered. Because it was born in the thoughts of the Creator, it is not subject to human weakness and volatility.

Hashem in His Lovingkindness empowers each individual to shape his own life, especially by allowing us to choose our own thoughts. He doesn't force us to do this, He gives each person free will. Each of us is able to choose, in large measure, what we think, feel and believe. But even though we are free to choose, in Judaism, unlike classical Western thought, we find certain areas in which we are *commanded* to think and feel a certain way, because God has determined that it benefits us (not Him, the Creator is without need of improvement.) We are even commanded to believe.

In the Shema, for example, we are commanded to love God with all our heart, soul and might. Various commentaries on the Shema reveal to us that there are actions by which we can show and express our feelings of love for God. For example, sincere prayer, which is referred to as the service of the heart, is one of the main ways in which Jews express love of Hashem "with all our heart."[4] When we express our heartfelt love of God through the act of praying (praying from a prayer book, making hitbodedut, the recitation of Psalms, and so on) the feelings of love we have for God are reflected back to us and strengthened. Rebbe Nachman of Breslov explains that in order for us to actualize our spiritual self, we must verbally express our yearning for a loving connection with God, asking Him to help us to have a relationship with Him.[5]

Another example of legislating how we think and feel can be found in the subtext of the first of the Ten Commandments: *I am the Lord your God who brought you out of Egypt, out of the house of slavery.*[6] We are commanded to recognize that Hashem is God, the Creator and Sustainer, who encompasses and fills all of Creation, to know him (to the best of our human ability), and to live with that awareness each day. In fact, this recognition is one of the Six Constant Mitzvot.[7]

What do I do if this doesn't feel relevant to me?

Where does this leave you if you understand that belief in the Mashiach is part of normative Judaism but you just don't "feel" it, you don't truly believe? The answer is: you're in a good starting place. The fact that you are reading about Mashiach and thinking deeply about Jewish beliefs, is a sign that you are open-minded. You are open to exploring the incredible teachings of Judaism, especially as they concern the Messiah, the future of the world and your personal stake in things. People always have various struggles with faith and belief. You are using your free will to choose to learn more.

What can you do to find knowledge and inspiration? Google it! Today there are a wide range of books, websites and social media with groups devoted to sharing authentic Torah wisdom both live and archived (see the suggested reading list in the back of this book.) You can also join an inspiring WhatsApp group with free daily mini-lessons. Visit BreslovWoman. org for more information and see Appendix B in this book. Much about Judaism is available in translation, including in English, Russian, Farsi, French, Spanish, and other languages. You can also, as Rebbe Nachman of Breslov suggests, look for examples of Hashem's intervention (Divine Providence) each day. Remind yourself that everything that happens ultimately comes from the one true Source—God the Creator. Build on this by reinforcing your emunah and remember that each day is a day on which Mashiach can potentially arrive.

CHAPTER FOUR

Who and what is the Mashiach? I want to understand what I am anticipating.

Are you wondering who Mashiach will be? You're in good company. At first, even Mashiach himself won't know that he's the Mashiach! Like Moshe Rebbeinu who led the Jewish people out of Egypt, it will take time for Mashiach to believe and accept that he is indeed, the redeemer who will lead us out of exile.[1] And like Moshe, he will remain concealed while we are in exile. He won't be fully revealed until the end of exile and the arrival of the Geulah.[2]

It's important to keep in mind that the Mashiach is a human being like you and me, and is not a supernatural being. He is born of human parents with a specific family background. But before we discuss the family genealogy of Mashiach, we will discuss his spiritual genealogy. For that, we'll go back in time to Genesis and the creation. The Torah tells us that God's Spirit hovered over the face of the waters.[3] Several important texts discuss the meaning of this beautiful Torah verse, teaching that it alludes to the Melech HaMashiach, the King Messiah. In other words, the spirit of Mashiach was created at the very beginning, before time.[4]

The Mashiach's names reflect his greatness and life-mission. What is Mashiach's name? The Talmud discusses the various names that Mashiach might be called, including Shiloh, Yinnon, Chanina and Menachem.[5] Other names such as Yehuda and Nechemia are also mentioned. Like Mashiach, Moshe himself had several names (Tovia, Yekutiel, Avigdor, etc.) which reflected his greatness and life mission: to shepherd the Jews out of Egypt and bring us the Torah.* There are other threads that bind Mashiach to Moshe, too. Moshe was the greatest prophet who ever lived, and as such, is the root soul of Mashiach.

What is the life mission of Mashiach?

We'll discuss Mashiach's mission throughout this mini-book but let's take a moment to explore how absolutely vital to the Geulah is the Mashiach. Understanding the mystical mission of the Mashiach will lay the foundation for understanding why he's needed. The numerical value of the Hebrew word "Mashiach" gives us hints to the mission of Mashiach. The gematria of Mashiach (40+300+10+8) and nachash (50+300+8) are both 358. Identical numerical values reveal a relationship between two words and concepts,

------

* Your Jewish name—whether it is Hebrew, Yiddish, Ladino—also reflects your potential greatness and life-mission.

in this case, the Mashiach and the nachash, the serpent from the Garden of Eden. In the story, the snake tempts Eve to eat the fruit of the Tree of Knowledge of Good and Evil, which God had placed off limits to her and Adam. The midrash tells us the serpent spoke lashon hara (evil speech) about Hashem, telling Eve that he forbade that fruit because he didn't want human beings to be able to compete with Him![6]

The snake encouraged Eve to question the limits placed on a human being. The equivalent gematria of the snake and the Mashiach alludes to the teaching of the mystics who explain that "When the evil snake will be removed from the world, the holy snake will rule." In other words, the yetzer hara (the evil inclination) is the negative energy embodied by the Biblical snake who corrupted Eve. This negative inclination throws off any kinds of healthy boundaries or limits. Eventually, this evil profane snake energy will be transformed to positive, holy energy by the Mashiach. His is a mission of transformation.

Rebbe Nachman of Breslov points out a connection between the snake and evil speech. Evil speech includes lying, sarcasm and mockery, humiliating others, gossip and slander, and most especially gossip and slander about the Tzaddikim. The snake lured Eve with his evil speech, lying to her about Hashem's intentions, slandering Him. Whenever a person uses any kind of degenerate speech, especially speaking negatively about or unkindly to others, he is fueled by the energy of the evil snake. But Mashiach will eradicate evil. He will transform the malevolent force of evil speech into pure speech, the kind of speech that radiates kindness and love between Jews and love for God. You don't have to wait until the arrival of the Mashiach to join him in his mission: Giving others the benefit of the doubt, not speaking ill of them, speaking gently—these are ways in which each of us can begin our personal transformation and start to express the positive energy of the Mashiach right now.

What is Mashiach's family history?

Because the Mashiach is a human being, he has a normal human ancestry. The Bible says: "A shoot will sprout from the stock of Jesse, and a branch will grow from his roots." (Isaiah 11:1). Mashiach is that Davidic shoot. He must be a descendant of King David, who was the son of Jesse. There are Jewish families today who can trace their ancestry to King David. Learning a bit about King David's background can help us understand more about the Mashiach as well as his mission to transformation the negative snake-energy.

The term "Mashiach" means the anointed one. In Biblical times, the kings of Israel were anointed with oil poured from a horn. The prophet Samuel was the one who anointed David, making him king.[7] In order to do so, he traveled to Bethlehem to seek out the person Hashem wanted him to anoint, and eventually discovered that the one chosen by God was David. David was the son of Jesse and Nitzevet. David was shunned by his family because Jesse suspected David wasn't his legitimate son (he was legitimate, Jesse had made a mistaken judgment.) Because of this, David was made to eat alone, apart from his father and brothers, and spent much of his time out in the fields working as a shepherd. There he meditated and prayed in peace, with only his flock to keep him company.

David's father Jesse himself had problematical ancestry. His ancestors were Judah and Tamar. Tamar, who had been married to two of Judah's sons, both of whom died because of their egregious marital behavior, posed as a prostitute in order to conceive a child with Judah. That child was Perez. The book of Ruth outlines the generations from Perez to King David.[8] David's grandfather was Obed, the son of Boaz and Ruth the holy convert. Ruth was a Moabite princess who had converted to Judaism, and whose marriage to Boaz was questioned due to her background.[9] The Moabites were an enemy nation that descended from the union of Lot (of Sodom and Gomorrah infamy) and one of his daughters. The union with Lot's other daughter produced the Ammonites, another enemy of the Jews. How can a holy Tzaddik such as the Mashiach come from such a flawed family background?

The answer is profound. We can see that Mashiach coming from the Davidic line actualizes the idea that negative, profane energy will be transformed to positive, holy energy by the Mashiach. The evil union of Lot and his daughter, the unusual behavior of Tamar, Ruth's Moabite ancestry—all were darkness waiting to be transformed into light. And today, it's not difficult to see that the battle between light and darkness, good and evil is raging.

We can also spot a way in which Hashem is preparing society to accept, even embrace, the power of this transformation. Throughout most of history, people world-wide were limited by the circumstances of their birth. It was the exception to the rule that an individual could "make something of himself." In many societies, such as those under communist rule, there was nearly no way a person could "rise up" unless he was willing to live a life of corruption and deception. Beginning in what we might call the era of "freedom revolutions" in the 1700s (during the Industrial, French, and American revolutions), social mobility became not only possible but widespread in many places. Limits and boundaries to self-actualization, spiritual expression and material success were broken down. Yet, on the negative side, some protective limits were destroyed too. These revolutions challenged and changed the way humanity viewed the individual, no longer as cogs in the wheel, but instead as autonomous beings deserving of liberty by right of being born human.

Of course, Judaism has always embraced the power of personal development of the individual. Long before the era of "Give me liberty or give me death", the "self-made man", and motivational speakers, Judaism emphasized again and again the concept of individual freedom of choice and free will.

It seems like world events, especially those that have broken down rigid systems (for good and bad), have been preparing us for the times of Mashiach. With quarantines and shut-downs, we have been forced to spend more time alone, journeying inwards. You might even have discovered tremendous possibilities for self-development, including spiritual growth, during these difficult times.

Rebbe Nachman of Breslov is famous for saying to his followers that he didn't attain his great spiritual heights because of his illustrious family background (the holy Baal Shem Tov was his great grandfather), but rather, he achieved what he did through vision, will and desire, commitment and hard work. His advice rings true for us today: If you work as hard on yourself as the Tzaddikim did, you, too, can achieve great spiritual success. You can use your free will to move forward.

Someone once asked Rebbe Nachman what was the definition of free will. He said that free will is in the hands of a person. If he wants, he does, and if he doesn't want, he doesn't do.[10] Free will is the ability you have to act entirely as you wish.[11] In other words, whatever your background, whatever your situation, you can choose who you want to be. No one will reveal this liberating concept better to us than the Mashiach. He will truly empower us to choose.

In addition to lineage, what are the signs that the Mashiach is the genuine Mashiach?

The Rambam teaches us what to look for: Should there arise a king from the house of David, one who studies and follows the Torah like King David did, who lovingly teaches the Jewish people about their holy inheritance of Torah, who fights the battles for Godliness in this world—we can assume he is the Mashiach. And if he did all that and was successful, and he built the Holy Temple [in Jerusalem] on its site [the Temple Mount] and gathered together the dispersed Jewish people, then he is definitely the Mashiach. He will (then) heal the entire world [and teach us to connect to and] serve God together, as is written: "For then I shall teach the nations a pure language, and everyone will be able to call upon the name of God to worship him as one." (Zephania 3:9) [12]

<table>
<tr><td>

It's helpful to view Rambam's statements in a list:

1. Mashiach will have lineage traceable to King David

2. Like King David, he will be genuinely learned in Torah and fully embrace its precepts—he'll "talk the talk and walk the walk"

3. He will show the Jewish people who they really are, how to connect to Hashem and will encourage us to live a life of deeper meaning and fulfillment

4. He will battle atheism and immorality, and be victorious

5. Mashiach will gather in Jews dispersed around the world

6. He will build the Holy Temple of Jerusalem on the Temple Mount

</td><td>

How do we know he isn't the Mashiach? The next part of Rambam's discourse says that if he:

1. Doesn't succeed at these endeavors or

2. Is killed (dies) before he succeeds then we will know that he is not the Mashiach.

</td></tr>
</table>

Is there only one Mashiach?

In each generation there is a person who is potentially Mashiach. But we also learn that there are two Mashiachs, one referred to as Mashiach ben Yosef (Messiah son of Joseph) and the other Mashiach ben David (Messiah son of David). (According to another opinion, there is possibly just one Mashiach who will embody these two phases of spiritual development and expression.) We are taught that Mashiach ben Yosef will come first, will fight many battles, and will eventually be killed in the final war. Next, Mashiach ben David will come. Further discussion is beyond the scope of this book but keep in mind that there are several opinions on the way in which the Mashiach ben Yosef and Mashiach ben David will be revealed.

Will all people recognize and accept the Mashiach?

Not necessarily. There will likely be controversy, conflict and infighting, as to whether or not the Mashiach is genuine, though we hope not. However, if at that time we ourselves are unable to discern the truth, we can look to holy Torah scholars to advise us. True Torah sources and Tzaddikim will be here to point the way.

What can you do to learn more about who the Mashiach will be? Begin by reading a variety of authentic Jewish sources. Although the Rambam himself says we shouldn't focus to much on the details of Mashiach or the Messianic age, if this subject inspires you to come closer to Judaism, then it may be beneficial to you to learn a bit more. Perhaps the reason that today there is a plethora of information, including conflicting information, on this topic so central to Judaism, is in order to increase everyone's desire to seek truth and come closer to Hashem. It's a time of intense preparation.

CHAPTER FIVE

When and how will the Redemption occur?

The process of Mashiach's revelation and arrival has captured the attention of people worldwide The Rambam himself says that we shouldn't focus too much on the details of the Messianic era. We should instead work on our relationship with Hashem. Though this advice is helpful, reviewing some additional details can draw us to thinking about and yearning for the Messianic age, and this can open our hearts to Hashem and His Torah.

When is Mashiach coming?

According to the Sages, the world as we know it will last 6000 years (although the Redemption can happen sooner.)[1] The first 2000 years were characterized by chaos. The second 2000 years were characterized by Torah (beginning with the birth of Abraham in 1948 years from creation.) The last 2000 years, the period in which we now live, are referred to as the time of "the coming of the Mashiach."[2] Now, in 2021, we are in the year 5781. There are 220 years left on the Redemption clock. However, Mashiach can come anytime: "Though he tarries, wait for him, for he will surely come, it will not delay."[3]

Today, most Torah authorities agree: Mashiach will be revealed at any moment. Literally. All our sages say he, in fact, should have come already. Mashiach's arrival is imminent.

What is the war of Gog and Magog?

Gog and Magog are the names of anti-Semitic and anti-God nations and the war itself is spoken about by the prophets.[4] Ezekiel teaches: "And it will come to pass on that day, when Gog comes against the land of Israel, declares the Lord God, that My blazing indignation will flame in My nostrils. For in My jealousy and in the fire of My wrath I have spoken; Surely there shall be a great noise on that day in the land of Israel. And at My presence, the fishes of the sea and the birds of the heaven and the beasts of the field and all the creeping things that creep upon the earth and all the men who are upon the surface of the earth shall quake, and all the mountains shall be thrown down, and the cliffs shall fall to the ground."[5]

The Holy Zohar alludes to the war of Gog and Magog and says it will occur after the Mashiach comes. It will be a war against Israel (the Holy Land and the Jewish people) and Gog and Magog will incite other nations to join them. Three times there will be a war of Gog and Magog. The Chofetz Chaim, who passed away in 1933, said that World War I (1913-1918) was the first war of Gog and Magog. He foresaw another war far, far worse than World War I about 25 years after. This of course was World War II (1939 -1945) and the holocaust. He said the third war of Gog and Magog would come at some point after World War II, but didn't give a timeframe.

How long will this war last? Some say the final war will be over in a moment, others say it will unfold over time. Many say we are already in the midst of Gog and Magog. There are conflicting opinions on the details of the timing of the third war as it relates to Mashiach's arrival. We are taught that Elijah the Prophet will announce Mashiach's impending arrival three days ahead of time. Some say Elijah will instead announce the war of Gog and Magog which will happen before Mashiach comes. Some say the war comes after. However, we know Mashiach will be involved in many battles. But are the battles physical? While some may be, Rebbe Nachman teaches us that "Mashiach will conquer the world without firing a single bullet."[6] In fact, he tells us that Mashiach's main weapon is prayer.[7]

There are also opinions that the War of Gog and Magog is also not a physical war, but a war of technology or even simply a spiritual one. If so, it isn't a far stretch to see that this war is being waged now, on many fronts. The prophesies may be read allegorically but most agree that the descriptions refer to a physical war. Still, we can at the same time find a spiritual lesson in these descriptions and enrich our understanding and response to this prophecy. We can understand that Gog and Magog are forms of negative spiritual energies that have joined forces to weaken our emunah and cause depression and despair. *But we must fight back!* Rebbe Nachman teaches that there is no (genuine reason for) despair in the world at all. There is no hopeless case. He encourages us to strengthen ourselves—no matter how dark things seem in our personal lives or in the world at large. If we have faith in God, faith in our Tzaddikim, and faith in ourselves, we can get through anything.

What will the times be like before Mashiach comes?

The Talmud teaches that any generation in which the Holy Temple in Jerusalem isn't rebuilt, it's as if it was being destroyed.[8] What destroyed the Holy Temple? The first Temple was destroyed because of idol worship, immoral relationships, and bloodshed. The second Temple was destroyed because of sinat chinam, baseless hatred, the tell-tale sign of which is evil speech about others. In other words, hatred of other Jews is equal to the sins of idolatry, immorality and murder! The Chofetz Chaim tells us that this is precisely why it's so important that we should improve our speech.[9]

The sages disagree on some of the important details about when Mashiach will come and what the state of the world and the Jewish people will be. They say[10]:

There is a set time for Mashiach's arrival.

There is no set time for Mashiach's arrival.

He will come in the time when every Jew is completely innocent.

He will come in the time when every Jew is completely corrupt.

What we can be sure of is that our personal spiritual efforts are vital to the redemption and will affect how Mashiach comes[11]:

If the Jewish people merit it, Mashiach will
come with clouds of Heaven.

If they don't, he will come in a lowly way, riding on a donkey.

Virtually all Torah authorities agree: We are living in the times when Mashiach is on the horizon. Some of the signs of the "birth pangs of the Mashiach" are[12]:

Chutzpah (insolence and disrespect) will increase dramatically.

Everything will be very expensive.

We will see that our leaders (politicians and even some so-called religious leaders) will be atheists or will ignore God.

The places our sages used to meet will have become places of promiscuity.

People will view with disgust and disrespect those who believe in and live with Torah values.

Youth will brazenly disrespect adults, children will shame and brazenly stand against their parents.

The truth (about any important matter in this world) will be very hard to ascertain, as is currently the case.

And Mashiach will come[13]:

When the Holy Land of Israel will grow abundant produce.

When the Jewish people experience an inundation of troubles and distress like a river.

Does this sound like today's times? Many of our greatest sources, including the Chofetz Chaim, the Vilna Gaon, the Ramchal and others, teach that the period leading up to Mashiach will be one of great hardships, during which troubles will appear faster and faster, like the contractions of a woman in labor. The Chofetz Chaim says that troubles will begin to speed up back to back, so there will be no breathing room between the tribulations. We can expect difficulties to come like a deluge, which can only be withstood with simple faith, as this story by Rebbe Nachman illustrates:

The King's Hunt

A king once went hunting with his royal retinue. Suddenly a heavy rain fell. It was a deluge. In the confusion, his ministers forgot about him and scattered in all directions. The king was in great danger from the flood. He was all alone. He searched the forest until he found the cottage of a woodcutter. The man invited the king in and lit the stove. He offered the king a bowl of warm kasha. After he finished eating, he led the king to a bed on the floor made of straw. This was a very sweet, new experience for the king. He was so tired and exhausted it seemed as if he had never before had such a pleasurable sleep.

The next morning the rain stopped. The royal ministers and advisors went out to search for the king. They finally found him inside the woodcutter's cottage. They wanted him to return to the palace with them. "You did not even try to rescue me," said the king. "Each one of you ran to save himself. This simple man," he said pointing to the woodcutter, "rescued me. Here, in his modest cottage, he graciously served me dinner and gave me a warm bed. I had the sweetest experience. Therefore, he is the one who will bring me home, in his wagon. He will sit with me on my throne."[14]

Rebbe Nachman said that in the times before Mashiach comes, there will be a flood of atheism and immorality. This flood will cover all the high mountains, even the mountains in the Holy Land where the original flood did not reach. This time the deluge will come with such strength that the waters will splash over all the land. The flood will have an effect on even good and pure hearts. The Rebbe teaches that there is no way we can combat this flood with sophistication. *We must embrace simplicity and straightforwardness, and simple and straightforward wisdom and faith.*

Today, all the world's ministers and advisors have scattered. They're looking after themselves, running for their lives. The only ones who are able to battle this flood are the simple people, those with faith. Simplicity is the key to faith and the key to the Redemption. Simple people will be the ones sitting near the King on His Throne.

How can you grow your soul-connection to Judaism and your Jewish identity? These turbulent times mirror many ancient prophecies, on both a national and personal level. Studying the Hebrew Bible, Tanakh (the Torah/5 Books of Moses, the Prophets, the Holy Writings) as well as learning more about your psychospiritual self by studying the wisdom of Rebbe Nachman of Breslov's teachings are ways in which you can discover your soul-connection to your Jewish identity. If you are motivated to act on improving your speech, or are just curious about what Judaism has to say about this important subject, there are translations of all of Rabbi Yisrael Meir Kagan's works, including the sefer Chofetz Chaim. For more stories and parables related to the Mashiach, Jewish self-development, and Jewish mysticism, Rebbe Nachman's stories are available in translation. Also see suggested reading at the end of this book.

CHAPTER SIX

Where do we go from here?

*How should I prepare for what may likely be a very
sudden arrival of the Mashiach and the Redemption?*

It is said that the Chofetz Chaim (Rabbi Yisrael Meir Kagan) truly anticipated and believed that Mashiach would come any moment, so much so he had a special suit prepared, and kept a bag packed and ready for the move to the Holy Land. If he heard a loud noise or disruption, he often assumed this was heralding the arrival of the Mashiach. (It's said that Elijah will sound a blast on the shofar to herald the Mashiach's arrival.) The Chofetz Chaim's many followers testified that he spoke constantly about the urgent need for Jews to bring an awareness of Mashiach into the world.

Interestingly enough, though this saintly Jew authored many important scholarly works, he is known by the name of his most famous work, Chofetz Chaim,[1] which is a masterful guide to…the Jewish laws of good speech! Specifically, it's a user-friendly manual on how to avoid evil speech. It focuses on explaining the Jewish laws associated with looking at others with a "good eye" and speaking well of them. In other words, this incredible book shows specific steps we can take to turn the evil snake energy into holy energy. It's not too far of a stretch to say we can view his book as a significant how-to guide to help us ready the world—and ourselves—for Mashiach.

Related to this is Rebbe Nachman of Breslov's teaching that if we want to actively bring the spirit of Mashiach down into this world, we should work on breaking any anger.[2] Not getting angry is considered a vital element of spiritual self-mastery, a tremendous psychospiritual accomplishment. Also, the sages tell us that increasing our good deeds, the mitzvot that we do, helps pave the way for the Redemption, as does prayer. Especially keeping the Shabbat, because the Shabbat is equivalent to all the mitzvot together. The power of Shabbat is so great that even if someone worships idols, if he keeps the Shabbat, he will be forgiven.[3] Also, keeping the Shabbat rescues a person from the oppression of exile—it makes life in general, sweeter.[4] And if the Jewish people would keep the Shabbat with all its observances two consecutive times, the redemption would come immediately.[5]

The delights of the Geulah are tempting, but it seems like there is so much to learn. What can I do if I want to progress without being overwhelmed?

When you were in the womb, angels taught you the entire Torah. But the moment before you were born, an angel slapped you and you forgot everything.[6] What to do about it? Be open to learning what you've forgotten. The Tikkunei Zohar teaches that the reason a Jew learns

Torah in the womb is that the experience adds vitality to the Torah learning he'll do in his lifetime. *Jewish wisdom is your birthright.*

Learn more about the Mashiach, the Geulah and other genuine Jewish concepts. Pursue genuine Torah knowledge for even a few minutes a day. Rebbe Nachman of Breslov says: A little bit is also good.

What is important to keep in mind as you learn? An essential fact of all effective education, especially Torah education, is realizing that the more you learn, the more you'll come to see that there is so much you don't know. The greatest and most brilliant scholars in our proud history of Jewish education were actually very humble. That's because all their studying brought them to recognize the unfathomable, unquantifiable greatness of God and His Love for each Jew. It will be the same for you. The more you explore genuine Jewish wisdom, the more you will be able to connect to the beauty of being a Jew. Simply put: The more you learn, the more you'll be able to make Jewish wisdom a part of you. After a while, your learning will give you a fresh appreciation of the details of your personal life story, as well as the material and spiritual history of the Jewish people. *Jewish wisdom is your legacy.*

Also, keep in mind the importance of strengthening your emunah. Faith is crucial to your psychospiritual self-actualization. When you reach the limits of your intellectual understanding, that is when emunah must kick in. When you reach the boundaries of human intellect, emunah is the mechanism which will bring you to a new level of understanding. Emunah provides a kind of deep knowing that is more encompassing than the knowledge you gain from book learning and life-experiences alone. When your emunah is developed, and you then engage in book learning, you will experience a multi-modal knowledge, knowledge that has the potential to express itself in a variety of meaningful ways. Your perspective changes, and life's ups and downs become less scary. It is as if emunah adds another dimension to your sight. It might even be called the sixth sense.

If you ask if you are truly capable of this, know that faith is a latent Jewish talent. Each of us is born with the potential to develop emunah. You were born with this faculty. It's in your Jewish spiritual DNA. Our sages teach that God doesn't ask anything of a person he cannot do—therefore, emunah is something *you are definitely able to achieve*. All it takes is your will, as Rebbe Nachman says: If you want, you'll do. Nothing will stand in your way.

What is the main thing to focus on? Perhaps the most important ingredient of all is joy. Choosing to share joy with others and yourself. To take delight in the special moment in your life. To feel the joy of Shabbat, family and friends. Happiness is a choice. Coming closer to Hashem is a choice. Preparing for Mashiach and the Geulah are choices. May you be blessed to choose wisely.

ACKNOWLEDGMENTS

Thank you to Ella (Esther) Gurevich, my dear friend and student, who initiated this project and invited friends and family of Dr. Eleonora Goudis, to participate. Thank you to my dear friend and student, Dr. Eleonora Goudis, whose generous contribution to the printing of the previous, limited-edition of this book made the entire Mashiach project possible—may it be an *aliyah* for the *neshama* of her beloved mother, Chana bat Ephraim, to whom this book is dedicated. Thank you to everyone who helped us distribute copies of the first edition. Thank you to Shulamit Michal Strassburger for her volunteering and for her meticulous attention to detail (and patience) – by keeping our lists updated, she enabled hundreds of people to receive their copies of this book. Thank you to Simcha Yael Roth who proofread an early draft of the text and made many helpful corrections. Also, thanks to Yocheved Stock for her artistic advice on the cover. So many teachers have inspired this and other Breslov Woman projects and I'm grateful to them (only some are listed here): R' Chaim Kramer of the Breslov Research Institute and his wife, Gita, R' Nasan Maimon of BreslovTorah.com, R' Noson Ephraim Kenig, R' Yitzchak Meir Morgenstern, R' Yaakov Meir Shechter, Rebbetzin Tzipporah Heller, R' Nissan Dovid Kivak, R' Avraham Tzvi Kluger, and

R' Yitzchak Ginsburgh. Thank you to R' Avraham Greenbaum of Azamra.org for his generosity and allowing me to use his literary translations of Rebbe Nachman's stories in my books and classes. Thank you to R' Meir Elkabas, an inspirational and dedicated Breslov teacher and friend, for taking the time to read and review this book. Many thanks are due to Gavriel and Chana Sneider. As the President of the Board of Breslov Woman, Chana generously supports Breslov programs and publications. Her sage editorial advice and tough questions made this book more readable and meaningful. She also did much of the hard work of distributing first edition and as well as added her creative color-flair to the text on the cover of this edition. Thank you to my beloved students who keep me on my toes and inspire me to keep on sharing Rebbe Nachman's teachings. I spent half a year gathering a massive quantity of research materials and making copious color-coded notes about the huge subjects of Mashiach and the Geulah. The biggest problem in putting this book together was one of scope, how to decide what was essential to an introduction to Mashiach, and what could and should be left out. Many thanks to my husband, Moshe Chaim, who made valuable recommendations about what to include and gave laser-sharp advice about how to organize the material (and who rescued me from four very tall piles of research materials.) Any errors or omissions are entirely my own. Thank you to the *Tzaddik Emes*, Rebbe Nachman ben Fayga, for teaching me *simcha*, *emunah* and the importance of "holy *chutzpah*". Thank you to *Hashem* for everything.

Chaya Rivka Zwolinski, Second Edition, May 2021

APPENDIX A

Glossary of Hebrew Terms

Aliyah lit. "going up", here refers to moving to the Land of Israel (going up to the Holy Land)

Beit Hamikdash the Holy Temple in Jerusalem (refers to the first, second and upcoming third Temple)

Chutzpah brazenness, impudence

Emunah faith

Gedolim great rabbis, Torah authorities

Gematria the Hebrew language is the holy tongue the Holy One used to create the world, therefore embedded in each word and letter are layers of mystic codes, gematria is the name for several systems of determining hidden meanings in the words and letters by numeric code

Geulah world redemption and the arrival of Mashiach

Hashem lit. "the name", a way to refer to God by the Holy Name without using the name indiscriminately

Hashgacha pratit Divine Providence, Hashem's never-ending comprehensive, supervision of everything *in creation*

Hitbodedut talking to Hashem in your own words, in private, as you would a best friend; prayerful meditation; Rebbe Nachman emphasized the importance of hitbodedut and taught that it was central to achieving spiritual growth

Kotel the last standing wall, the Western wall of the Beit Hamikdash, the holiest site in Judaism, where the Shechina never has left

Lashon Hara lit. Evil Speech, often referring to various forms of gossip (both true and untrue), but may refer to other types of forbidden speech

Lecha Dodi this ethereal liturgical poem, which welcomes the Shabbat as a beloved bride, written by Shlomo Alkabetz, a 16th century kabbalist from Tsfat, is part of the Kabbalat Shabbat (welcoming the Sabbath) service, and is set to a variety of beautiful melodies which vary according to community

Mashiach lit. anointed, the Messiah

Melech HaMashiach the King Messiah (he will be anointed as the King of Israel)

Midrash in general, this refers to portions of the Oral Torah (Talmud) that are interpretations, ethical, legal or mystical discussions, of the Written Torah, many in the form of stories

Mitzvot the commandments of the Torah, of which there are 613 (each of which may contain various components and laws); colloquially people refer to a "good deed" as a mitzvah, as well

Nachash serpent, especially the snake in the Garden of Eden, that embodied the yetzer hara (the evil inclination)

Nekuda tova lit. good point, may be used as shorthand for the Godly soul

Neshama general term for the Jewish soul

Olam Haba lit. the World to Come, may refer to either the life after this one (Heaven, etc.) and/or the time of Mashiach and the Geulah

Sanhedrin often refers to the main "Great Court", a religious court composed of 71 of Israel's most brilliant and righteous sages, which met in the Beit Hamikdash, which was essential to the functioning of this court; once the Temple was destroyed, the Sanhedrin was dissolved

Sefer book, often refers to a holy text

Shechina the hidden, feminine-aspect of Hashem also called the Divine Presence, She is in exile with us and will dwell once again in the times of Mashiach; today, the Shechina remains in one unique place: the Kotel still standing in Jerusalem

Siddur Jewish prayer book

Sinat chinam baseless hatred

Talmud nearly 3000 double-pages long, the Talmud is largely comprised of the Mishna, the Oral Law which was first written down in the 2nd century CE, and the Gemara, rabbinic discussions and commentary; it is the guide for living life as Jew and offers discussions of Jewish law, customs, Jewish thought and ethics, history, stories, and much more, much of Midrash (textual commentary on law and Biblical narrative) is also included

Tanakh Abbreviation for Torah (Chumash/Five Books of Moses), Nevi'im (Book of Prophets), and Ketuvim (Writings), also called the Hebrew Bible

Tikkun correction, remedy, usually spiritual

Tikkunei Zohar A significant Kabbalistic text, it contains seventy important commentaries on the first word of the Torah, "Breishit" (in the beginning)

Torah may refer to the Five Books of Moses and/or the scroll it is written on by a scribe; the Hebrew Bible (Tanakh); the combined texts of Jewish wisdom, especially the Tanakh, the Talmud, and often the Shulchan Aruch (codes of Jewish law) and the Kabbalah (the mystical texts); may also include works of Chassidut, Ethical/Moral, and other teachings; an individual lesson/the body of work of a sage and/or Tzaddik, especially Rebbe Nachman of Breslov's *Likutey Moharan*

Tzaddik/Tzaddikim sing./pl. a highly righteous individual devoted to serving Hashem and helping individuals come closer to Him, the tzaddik has a unique role in Jewish life

Yetzer hara the evil inclination, the impulse or desire to engage in thoughts, feelings or behaviors that conflict with Torah and our Godly soul

Zohar lit. radiance or splendor, the most studied Kabbalistic text, written by Shimon bar Yochai in the 2nd century, CE, it contains mystic discussions of God and creation, the nature of the soul, good and evil, and much more

APPENDIX B

Suggested Reading

By the author:

May You Have a Day: Making Every Day Better with the Teachings of Rebbe Nachman of Breslov, by Chaya Rivka Zwolinski, Breslov Woman, 2020 (Learn 120 Breslov mini-lessons on living life with more hope, joy and connection)

BreslovWoman.org (Website of Breslov Woman group, with event and class listings, article, videos, podcasts and more)

Jewish Scripture:

The Tanakh (The Hebrew Bible including the Chumash—Five Books of Moses, Prophets and Writings). A clearly translated, traditional version is Artscroll Mesorah Stone Edition; also see Sefaria.org; Chabad.org

The Chumash/Torah (The Five books of Moses). A beautiful translation by Rabbi Aryeh Kaplan, z'al, is published by Moznaim; also see Artscroll; Sefaria.org; Chabad.org

Tehillim (King David's Psalms which are also part of Tanakh). An ancient Jewish custom, one your ancestors certainly engaged in is reciting Psalms aloud, which is propitious for powerful personal salvations. You can find many translations or use the Tehillim app and website: Tehillim-online.com.

Teachings of the Tzaddikim:

Chofetz Chaim There are a several translations in a variety of languages of this moral masterpiece by Rabbi Yisrael Meir Kagan. Visit cchf.global for the Chofetz Chaim Heritage Foundation's website and bookstore.

Likutey Moharan Rebbe Nachman of Breslov's Magnum Opus containing hundreds of inspiring, challenging, and fascinating lessons on psychospiritual development, Jewish life, relationships, and more. Lesson 282 is called "Azamra", a fundamental teaching on how to believe in and find the good in yourself (and others.) The Breslov Research Institute (BRI) version with commentary is a masterpiece in its own right—a comprehensive, 15 volume set and BRI also publishes a pocket-book version of two lessons, Azamra and Ayeh (another key lesson.) Also highly recommended is Sippurey Maasiot (Rebbe Nachman's Stories) beginning with the first story, The Lost

Princess, which is about Mashiach and the Redemption on both the national and personal level.

General Breslov Study (in English)

You can learn more about Breslov teachings at my website BreslovWoman.org as well as my YouTube channel (Chaya Rivka Zwolinski.) Also, you can find more from me and other teachers at the website of BRI publishers, Breslov. org. For a user-friendly, comprehensive learning journey through Breslov teachings with Rav Nasan Maimon, visit BreslovTorah.com. Rabbi Avraham Greenbaum's warm and welcoming approach to Breslov learning is available at Azamra.org. Rabbi Meir Elkabas' compassionate psychospiritual teachings can be found at BreslovTherapy. blogspot.com. Visit Rabbi David Sears at BreslovCenter. blogspot.com for more advanced, intellectual Breslov study and information. For inspiring daily mini-lessons, classes and events, text your name to: 917-348-1573 and you'll be added to my Breslov WhatsApp group. I can also be reached at crzbreslov@gmail.com.

END NOTES

Chapter One: What will (my) life be like after Mashiach comes?

1. Isaiah 61:5

2. Isaiah 35:10

3. Yalkut Shimoni Remez 503

4. Isaiah 56:7

5. Exodus 25:8

6. Mishkney Elyon, Ramchal, translated as Secrets of the Future Temple by Rabbi Avraham Greenbaum

7. Shir HaShirim (Song of Songs) 2:9

8. Midrash Bamidbar Rabba 11:2 and Shemot Rabba 2:2

9. Isaiah 25:8

10. Isaiah 35:6-7

11. Psalms 71:20

12. Likutey Moharan, 282, "Azamra", Rebbe Nachman of Breslov

13. Likutey Halachot, Hashkamat Haboker, Halacha 1:8, Reb Noson of Breslov

14. Mishneh Torah, Laws of Kings, 12:5, Rambam and Isaiah 11:9

15. Tehillim (Psalms) 27:4

16. Tehillim (Psalms) 100:5

17   Devarim (Deuteronomy) 14:1

18   Devarim (Deuteronomy) 14:2

19   Shir HaShirim (Song of Songs), King Solomon. This beautiful, holy song from Tanakh describes the love between God and the Jewish people as the love between husband and wife.

Chapter Two: I'm interested in learning more about the Messiah, but I am more focused on the way things are going right now. Why should I think about the Mashiach when I really just want things to go back to the way they were?

1   The Book of Redemption, Ramban (Rav Moshe ben Nachman, Nachmanides)

2   Lecha Dodi (Come my Beloved), Rabbi Shlomo HaLevi Alkabetz

3   Talmud Brachot 57b

4   Likutey Moharan 193

5   Talmud Bava Batra 7b

6   Sippurey Maasiot, Rebbe Nachman's Stories

Chapter Three: I already believe in God. Is it necessary that I believe in Mashiach, too?

1   "Whoever does not believe in him or does not anticipate his coming, denies not only the other prophets but also the Torah and Moses." Mishneh Torah, Laws of Kings, 11:4, Rambam

2   The Thirteen Principles of Faith, Rambam (Rav Moshe ben Maimon, Maimonides), Found in most Siddurim after the morning prayers

3   Shaar HaKavanot, Arizal (Rav Yitzchak Luria

4   Talmud Taanit 2a

5   Likutey Moharan 31

6   Shemot (Exodus) 20:2

7   Shesh Mitzvot Temidiot is based on an anonymous 13th century Spanish work, Sefer HaChinuch (Book of Education). The constant mitzvot are: Know there is a God, Don't believe in other Gods, Believe in God's Oneness/Unity, Love God, Have Awe and Fear of God, Don't let your heart or eyes pull you away from God (and His Torah)

Chapter Four: Who and what is the Mashiach?
I want to understand what I am anticipating.

1   Chatam Sofer Al HaTorah, Rav Moshe Sofer

2   Sfas Emes, Rav Yehuda Aryeh of Gur

3   Breishit (Genesis) 1:2 "...and the spirit of God was hovering over the face of the water."

4   Midrash Breishit Raba 8:1; Baal HaTurim, Rav Yaakov ben Asher, "And the spirit of God was hovering" has the same gematria (numerical value) as "this is the spirit of the Messiah";

5   Talmud Bavli, Sanhedrin 98b

6   Breishit Raba,19:6

7   I Shmuel 16:12: God commanded [Samuel]: "Arise! Anoint him, for this is he.

8   Megillat Rut 4:18-22

9   Megillat Rut 1:4 & 1:16

10   Likutey Moharan II, 110

11   Likutey Moharan II, 54

12   Mishneh Torah, Laws of Kings, 11:4, Rambam

**Chapter Five: When and how will
the Redemption occur?**

1   Talmud Sanhedrin 97a

2   Talmud Sanhedrin 97a

3   Habbakuk 2:3

4   Ezekiel 38,39; Zecharia 14; Jeremiah 30; Daniel 11-12;
     Joel 4

5   Ezekiel 38:18-20 (See also Ezekiel 39 for a prophecy
     with more details.)

6   Siach Sarfey Kodesh

7   Likutey Moharan 2, Rebbe Nachman of Breslov

8   Talmud Yoma 9b

9   Shmirat Halashon, Guarding our Speech, Rabbi Yisra-
     el Meir Kagan (author of Chofetz Chaim)

10   Talmud Sanhedrin 98a

11   Talmud Sanhedrin 98a

12   Talmud Sotah 49b

13   Talmud Sanhedrin 98a

14   Adapted from Rabbi Avraham Greenbaum's transla-
     tion on Azamra.org, used with permission

Chapter Six: Where do we go from here?

1   Chofetz Chaim, title alludes to Psalm 34:13-14 "Who
     is the man who desires life, who loves to see good days?
     Guard your tongue from evil and your lips from speak-
     ing deceitfully."

2   Likutey Moharan II, 16

3   Talmud Shabbat 118b

4   Talmud Shabbat 118b

5   Talmud Shabbat 118b

6   Talmud Niddah 30 a-b